TOURING THE YOR

BOOK 2 — THE EAST

This guide book, which is the second in a Dales, contains exact but simple directions fo visits to such well known places as Fountains ... and Skipton with an exploration of the quieter dales and fells of this outstandingly beautiful area.

The Main Circle Route (Maps 1 – 11) shown on the Key Map opposite covers 130 miles, and is far too long for a leisurely day's journey. We have therefore included 'link routes' to break this up into smaller circles (see Key Map). Each route, being circular, may of course be started at any point suitable to you.

HOW TO USE YOUR BOOK ON THE ROUTE

Each double page makes up a complete picture of the country ahead of you. On the left you will find a one inch to the mile strip map, with the route marked by a series of dashes. Direction is always from top to bottom, so that the map may be looked at in conjunction with the 'directions to the driver', with which it is cross referenced by a letter itemising each junction point. This enables the driver to have exact guidance every time an opportunity for changing direction occurs, even if it is only 'Keep straight, not left!'

With mileage intervals shown, the driver should even have warning when to expect these 'moments of decision', and if a sign post exists we have used this to help you, with a 'Signposted . . .' column. However, some re-signing is always in progress, and this may lead to slight differences in sign marking in some cases...... So beware of freshly erected signs.

We have also included a description of the towns and villages through which you will pass, together with some photographs to illustrate the route.

To gain full enjoyment from your journeys be prepared to leave your car as often as possible. We have tried to lead you away from the busy main roads whenever possible, but in constricted hill country, this is not always possible to achieve. We have referred briefly in the text to the dangers of attempting remote hill walks, or climbing of any sort, without adequate experience or equipment, but if at the moment you possess neither, be not dismayed, for it is still possible to find the solitude enjoyed by earlier generations of visitors by walking only a few hundred yards from the roadside. Many of you will then wish to become more adventurous, and this is the time to seek further advice. May we suggest that you first call at one of the National Park Information Centres (at Clapham, Malham, Hawes, Sedbergh, Grassington or Aysgarth) for advice, and that you then purchase *The Peak and Pennines,* by W. A. Poucher and *A Pennine Way Companion,* by the unbeatable A. Wainwright. The relevant 1:50,000 Ordnance Survey Maps are of course another essential requisite, and the 1:25,000 Ordnance Survey *Outdoor Leisure Maps: No. 2 Yorkshire Dales, Western Area; No. 10 Yorkshire Dales, Southern Area; No. 30 Yorkshire Dales, Northern & Central Areas* are most useful. There are special footpath maps of Malham and Aysgarth available at the National Park Centres named above.

Do not try to cover too many road miles in one day, for there are so many wonderful opportunities for those who are really prepared to look about them...... limestone and gritstone heights, quiet woodlands, rock strewn streams, and the incomparable dales themselves. So drive slowly, stop often and take time off to absorb the spirit of this fascinating landscape and its warm hearted inhabitants.

COMPILED BY PETER, HELEN AND DAVID TITCHMARSH
REVISED BY ALLAN AND IRENE BLACKNALL
PHOTOGRAPHY BY ALAN AND PETER TITCHMARSH

Map 1

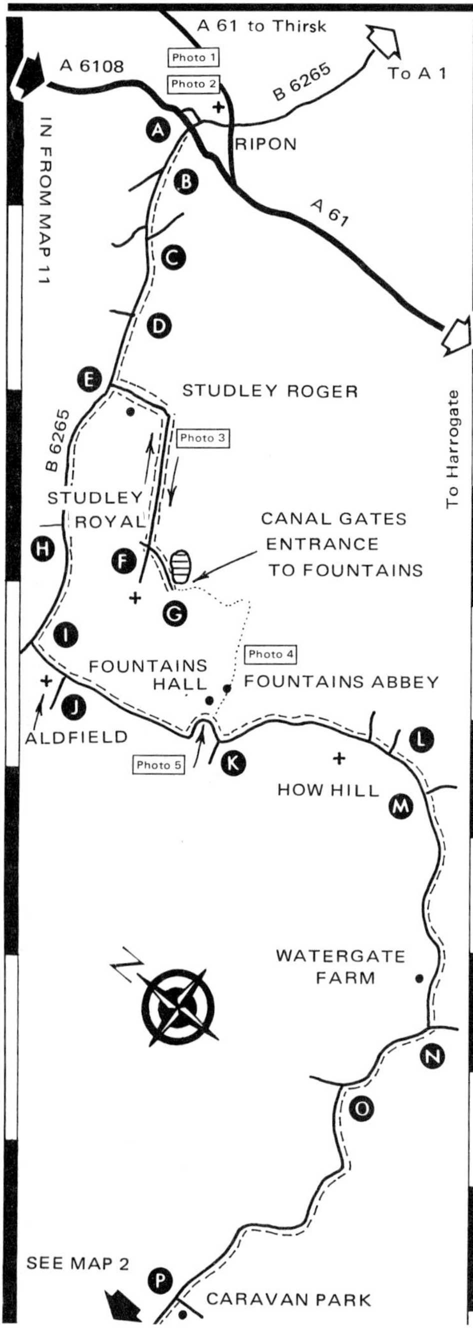

Ref.	Miles	Directions	Sign-posted
A		Leave South West corner of Ripon Market Square, on B6265, and... Keep Midland Bank on left (Keep straight out of Ripon on B6265)	Pateley Bridge
B	.5	Bear left at Y junction keeping on B6265	Studley Roayl
C	.3	Over off-set X rds., keeping on B6265, and... Over bridge	Studley Royal
D	.5	Straight, not right	Pateley Bridge
E1	.4	Turn left, off B6265	Studley Roger
	.1	Through Studley Roger	
	.3	Enter grounds of Studley Royal	
	.1	Through entrance portal, and along fine avenue with view of Studley Royal church at far end	
F1	.6	Bear left at diagonal X rds.	'Fountains Abbey'
G	.4	Arrive 'Canal Gates' car park for Fountains Abbey and... TURNABOUT into one way system after visiting Abbey	
	.3	Bear right at T junction	No sign
F2	.1	Over diagonal X rds., re-tracing our route...	Ripon
		View of Ripon Cathedral ahead	
	.7	Back through Studley Roger	
E2	.4	Turn left, re-joining B6265	Pateley Bridge
H	.8	Straight, not right, just beyond Studley Royal gates on left	No sign
I	.8	Bear left, off B6265	Fountains Abbey
J	.3	Straight, not right, by Aldfield church	Fountains Abbey
	.6	1 in 8 descent signed	
	.3	'West Entrance' to Fountains Abbey, and Fountains Hall on left	
	.1	Car Park on right	
K	.1	Fork left at Y junction	Markington
	.7	How Hill church ruins up to right	
L	.2	Straight, not left twice	No sign
M	.4	Straight, not left again	Ripley
	1.1	Watergate (farm) on right	
N	.3	Bear right at T junction	Sawley
O	.6	Turn left at T junction	Warsill
P	1.8	Straight, not left, by entry to Warren House Caravan Park	No sign
		Total mileage on this map: 12.8	

On Route

Ripon

Busy market town with two main centres of interest, the Market Square and the Cathedral. The ever bustling Market Square is dominated by a 90′ obelisk, built in 1702 by John Aislabie, then Mayor of Ripon, and later to be Chancellor of the Exchequer. Looking out over the square is James Wyatt's handsome Town Hall, ornamented with the boldly lettered city motto. . . 'EXCEPT YE LORD KEEP YE CITTIE, YE WAKEMAN WAKETH IN VAIN'. The office of Wakeman was replaced by that of Mayor in 1604, but his 'night-watchman' duties have been carried out ever since by the Hornblower, who blows the Wakeman's Horn at each corner of the Market Square at 9 o'clock every evening. The medieval Wakeman's House is also situated in the square.

Ripon Prison and Police Museum is a small specialist museum housed in the former Victorian City Gaol, and traces the twin themes of prison and police service development.

continued on page 27

Studley Royal (NT)

John Aislabie was Chancellor of the Exchequer when the notorious 'South Sea Bubble' burst in 1720, and it was his dismissal and enforced retirement that was responsible for the glories of Studley Royal. We first come upon the East Gate, a handsome entrance leading to a long avenue of trees in a great deer park. This leads to the tall spired St. Mary's Church, which was designed in an elaborate Early English style by that great 'High Victorian' architect, William Burges, its flamboyance reminding the visitor of one of his other great masterpieces, Cardiff Castle. Its interior is well worth visiting and there are fine views eastwards, down a long avenue and across fields to Ripon.

The mansion was burnt out in 1945 and later demolished, and our chief debt must be to John Aislabie's son William, who purchased the Fountains Abbey estate in 1768 and laid out the magnificent series of canals, lakes, temples and woodlands in the valley between Fountains and the original park.

Fountains Abbey (NT)

We cannot stress too strongly. . . when visiting Fountains Abbey, park your car at the Canal Gates entrance (restaurant here), and walk up through the splendid gardens (about 1 mile). . . they are a delight in themselves and they provide a wonderfully contrived 'surprise view' of the abbey. . . set amongst wide lawns between opposing wooded slopes.

This great Cistercian abbey of Fountains was established in the 12th century and despite the aims of simplicity sought by the original 'colonizers' from York, it grew into one of England's richest monastic houses (due largely to its vast revenues from wool). Despite considerable robbery of stone, especially by the builder of Fountains Hall, a reasonable proportion

continued on page 5

Fountains Hall (see page 5)

1. *Aislabie Monument, Ripon*

2. *West towers, Ripon Cathedral*

3. *Entrance Portal, Studley Royal*

4. *Fountains Abbey*

5. *Fountains Hall*

Map 2

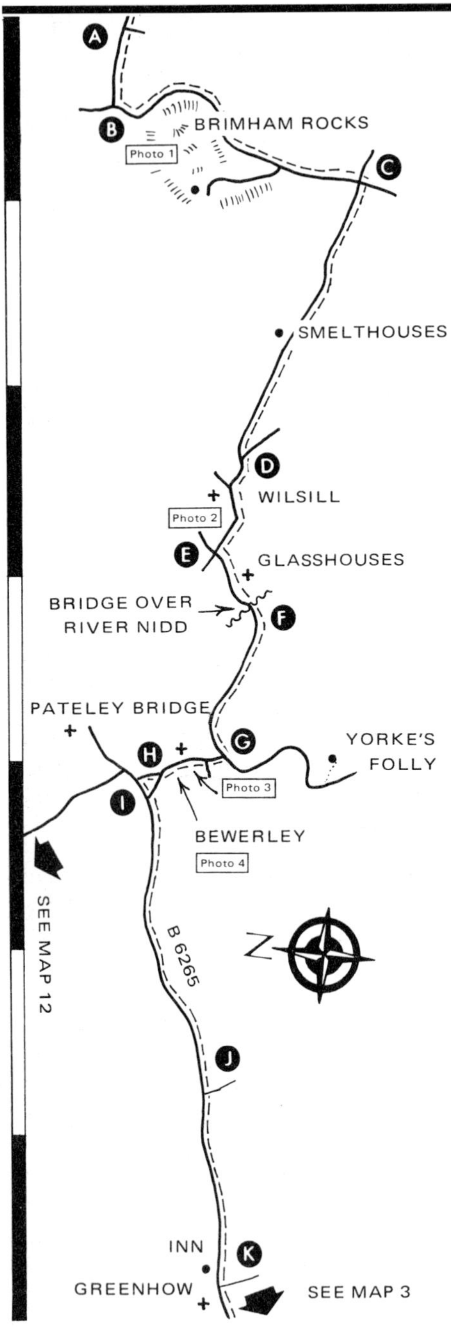

Ref.	Miles	Directions	Sign-posted
A	.2	Straight, not left	No sign
B	.9	Turn left at T junction	Brimham Rocks
		First of Brimham Rocks visible ahead	
	1.2	Straight, not right (But turn right to visit Brimham Rocks — .5 to parking area)	
	.3	Now leaving Brimham Rocks area	
C	.2	Turn right at X rds., and...	Smelthouses
		Down 1 in 6 hill Fine views of Nidderdale ahead	
	.3	1 in 7 descent signed	
	.5	1 in 6 descent signed	
	.4	Through Smelthouses hamlet	
D	.5	Bear right on to B6165 in Wilsill	Pateley Bridge
	.1	Straight, not right, at T junction by bridge, keeping on B6165	No sign
	.3	Birch Inn on right	
	.1	Glasshouses entry signed, and...	
E		Turn left, off B6165	Glasshouses
	.2	Pleasant green up to right, small church to left	
		Down steep hill	
	.2	Mill on left. Mill pound on right	
		Over River Nidd, and...	
F		Bear right beyond bridge	No sign
G	.9	Turn right, and over bridge (But turn left if you wish to look at Yorke's Folly — 1 mile)	Pateley Bridge
	.1	Straight, not left, and...	No sign
		Enter Bewerley	
	.1	Bewerley Grange chapel on right (Watch for this with care)	
H	.2	Straight, not left	No sign
I	.2	Turn sharp left, on to B6265, by the Royal Oak Inn (BUT TURN RIGHT IF YOU WISH TO START MAP 12, OR SIMPLY VISIT PATELEY BRIDGE) (Keep on B 6265 for 6 miles)	Grassington
	.2	Straight, not left, at Y junction	No sign
J	1.8	Straight, not left at T junction	No sign
	.6	Greenhow entry signed	
	.3	Miner's Arms Hotel on right	
K	.1	Straight, not left at T junction, and...	Grassington
		Church on right	
		Total mileage on this map: 9.9	

On Route

Fountains Abbey *continued from page 3*

of the structure remains, and from this we can obtain a most interesting picture of monastic life in medieval England.

Fountains Hall (NT)

Extremely handsome early Jacobean mansion built just outside the west gate of Fountains Abbey. Although on a more intimate scale, its elaborate front reminds us of Hardwick Hall in Derbyshire. The interior, with its fine panelling and elaborate plasterwork is a splendid example of Jacobean decoration.

Brimham Rocks (NT)

Fantastic, freakish, grotesque, weird . . . all the well worn epithets have been used to describe these gritstone outcrops extending over an area of fifty acres, now in the care of the National Trust. The erosive powers of wind, water and frost have, over millions of years, created some (dare we say it!) fantastic shapes. Explore at leisure amongst heather and bracken to find such 'works of nature' as The Leaning Tower, The Kissing Chair, The Turtle, The Knob and the Dancing Bear . . . to name but a few. There are also some enchanting views out over Nidderdale and the moors beyond; and an Information Centre, and Refreshment Kiosk.

Smelthouses

Minute hamlet beneath Brimham Moor, whose name reminds us that we are heading into old mining country. In the 18th century there was no doubt a smelting mill here for the processing of lead ore.

Glasshouses

Another village with pleasant views across Nidderdale, to wooded slopes crowned by Yorke's Folly, an 18th century 'eye-catcher' built to provide employment in hard times. We liked Glasshouses' spacious triangular green overlooked by trim cottages with colourful gardens.

Bewerley

Looks across the River Nidd to Pateley Bridge and has a lively inn, the Royal Oak, and a fascinating little 16th century chapel. This was built by Marmaduke Huby, last abbot of Fountains, and is attached to the grange (both lie behind a wall and the gate to the chapel is very easily missed). It has been beautifully restored, and with its stone flagged floors, open fireplace at the west end and open timbered roof, is well worth visiting.

Greenhow Hill

A bleak little village standing at over 1300′ above sea level and Yorkshire's highest village. The Miner's Arms Hotel and the pockmarked moorlands round about remind us that this was great mining country (from pre-Roman times until the late 19th century). The little Victorian church stands in a dank overgrown churchyard and is not of interest to visitors.

1. At Brimham Rocks

2. Wilsill

3. Bewerley Grange Chapel

4. Summer sunshine at Bewerley

Map 3

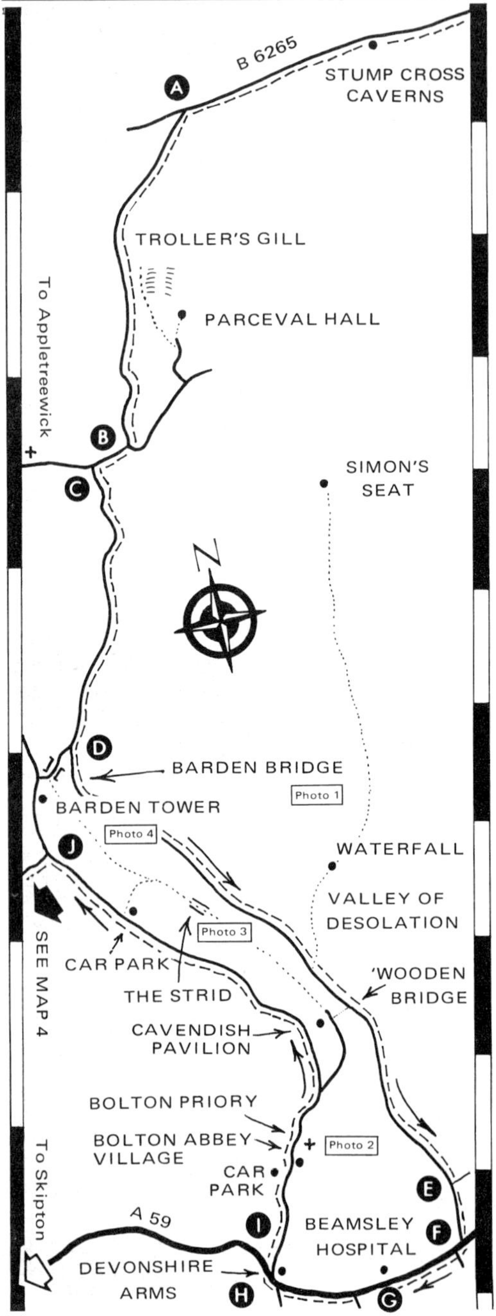

Ref.	Miles	Directions	Sign-posted
	1.7	Stump Cross Caverns on left	
A	1.3	Turn left, off B6265	Barden
	1.9	Down steep hill	
B	.2	Straight, not left at Y junction (But turn sharp left if you wish to visit Parceval Hall Gardens, and/or walk to Troller's Gill — .8)	Appletreewick
C	.3	Turn left at T junction	Barden
		Rocky heights of Simon's Seat up left	
	.6	Over bridge in small wooded valley (Now in Wharfedale)	
D	1.1	Fork left, up narrower road (But fork right, if you wish to visit Barden Bridge, or link on to Point J — .7)	Hazelwood
	1.4	Through gate beyond wood	
	.4	1 in 5 descent signed	
	.2	Over bridge crossing Posforth Gill	
	.1	Lovely views of Wharfe down to right, and path to Valley of Desolation on left	
	.2	Path to right, crossing "Wooden Bridge' to Cavendish Pavilion	
	.3	Through ford	
E	.5	Straight, not right by farm	No sign
	.1	Straight, not left by farm	No sign
	.2	Straight, not left by farm	Hazelbrook
F	.5	Turn right, with care, on to A59, and…	No sign
		Straight, not left	No sign
	.4	Beamsley Hospital (almshouses) on right	
G	.3	Straight, not left	Bolton Abbey
	.3	Over River Wharfe	
H	.1	Bear right, keeping on A59	
I	.2	Bear right, on to B6160 by Devonshire Arms	Grassington
	.3	Bolton Abbey entry signed	
		Car Park on left (Use this if you wish to walk to Priory)	
	.2	Through attractive archway	
		Bolton Priory visible to right	
	.3	Straight, not right by Cavendish Monument (But turn right if you wish to visit Cavendish Pavilion, etc.)	
	1.7	Car Park for Strid Wood Nature Trail on right	
J	.6	Turn left at T junction (But go straight ahead, if you wish to visit Barden Tower — .3)	Skipton
		Total mileage on this map: 15.7	

On Route

Stump Cross Cavern

This is an extensive cave system complete with stalactites and stalagmites, discovered by lead miners in the 1850's. Well worth visiting.

Parceval Hall

An old farmhouse, now the Bradford Diocesan House. The pleasant terraced gardens are possibly open to the public from Easter to the end of October. (Please check locally).

Troller's Gill

This dramatic limestone gorge may be viewed from a public footpath starting from the left of the road to Parceval Hall (immediately before crossing stream).

Barden Bridge

A fine 17th century bridge crossing the Wharfe below Barden Tower. There is a large car park and paths southwards down both sides of the river.

Valley of Desolation

It is possible to walk up this delightful valley, past the 50′ Posforth Gill waterfall, and up to the rocky summit of Simon's Seat (1532′).

Beamsley Hospital

17th century almshouses completed by that inveterate builder and restorer of castles and churches, Lady Anne Clifford, and incorporating a unique circular building centred upon a chapel.

Bolton Abbey Village

Small village with a large car park for visitors to the monastic ruin from which it takes its name. . . although this was in fact a priory.

Bolton Priory

The ruined priory, founded in 1120, is beautifully situated above the curving banks of the River Wharfe. The nave of the priory church had long been used as a parish church, and this was spared when the priory was dissolved in 1538. The gatehouse was also saved, and this was incorporated into 18th century Bolton Hall, which is one of the residences of the Duke of Devonshire.

The Cavendish Pavilion

Here is a cafe, restaurant and riverside picnic area, with the 'Wooden Bridge' giving pedestrian access to our road down the other side of the Wharfe. It is also possible to walk north from here along the gloriously wooded banks of the Wharfe to the Strid.

The Strid

Park .6 before Point J for the best access to the Strid (about 15 minutes walk). . . a narrow rocky cleft through which rush the waters of the Wharfe. Purchase the excellent leaflet to the Strid Wood Nature Walk at the car park hut. Fee payable for access.

Barden Tower

A tall fortified manor house, built by Henry Clifford about 1485, and now a gaunt ruin, romantically sited above the Wharfe. A tablet records that Barden was repaired by Lady Anne Clifford in 1658–59, but today the interior is too dangerous to explore (one can still walk around the outside).

1. Barden Bridge

2. Bolton Priory

3. The Strid

4. Barden Tower

Map 4

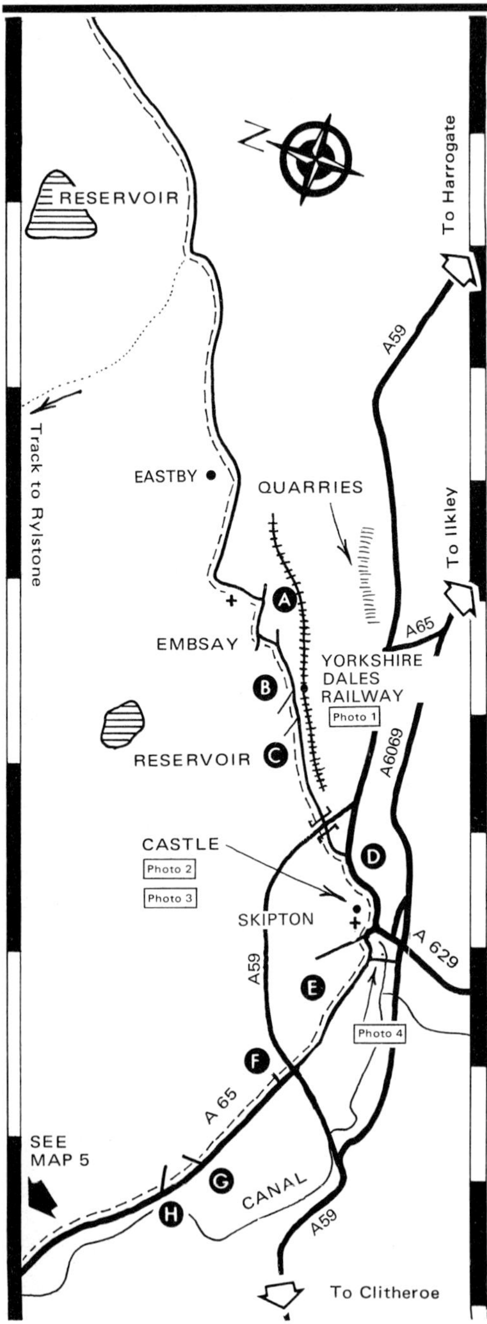

Ref.	Miles	Directions	Sign-posted
		On to Barden Moor	
	.7	Fine views back over Wharfedale	
	.4	Lower Barden Reservoir down to right, and track to Rylstone on right	
	.3	Fine views southwards	
	.7	1 in 7 descent signed	
	.2	Large quarry over to left	
	.1	Down hairpin bend	
	.1	Entering Eastby	
	.2	Mason's Arms on left	
	.6	Embsay entry signed	
	.2	Church on right	
A	.1	Turn right at T junction by Haw Bank House	Skipton
	.2	Bear left by large tree	Skipton
	.1	Bear right by paper shop	Skipton
B	.2	Straight not right But turn down left if you wish to visit Transport Museum, at old railway station)	No sign
	.1	Cavendish Arms on left	
C	.1	Straight, not right, and...	No sign
		Keep straight out of Embsay on the Skipton Road	
	.8	Skipton entry signed	
D	.1	Turn right with care on to A6131	Skipton
	.4	Castle up to right	
E	.1	Bear round to right at roundabout by church	Settle
	.1	Bear left at T-junction	Seattle
	.1	Car park and canal wharves over to left. Keep straight out of Skipton	
F	1.0	On to A65 at major roundabout	The Lakes & Kendal
	.1	Straight, not right	Settle
G	.3	Straight, not right	Settle
H	.2	Straight, not right	Settle
	.1	Leeds and Liverpool Canal over to left	
		Total mileage on this map: 7.8	

On Route

Barden Moor

Open moorland with fine views back over Wharfedale. There is a path over to Rylstone and Hetton (Map 5) known as the White Doe Track. . . about six miles (see Route Directions).

Eastby

A tidy terraced village looking southwards to Skipton Moor. No special features.

Embsay

A hard, dark grey stone village, with Victorian terrace houses looking across to the great quarries which have cut right through the spine of Haw Park Hill. The restored railway station at Embsay is the base of the Yorkshire Dales Railway, which offers its passengers a four-mile round trip hauled by a vintage steam locomotive. The trains have a licensed buffet car, and there is a buffet and bookshop at the station.

Skipton

From our point of view Skipton is a pleasant and compact town, with its church and castle at the northern end of the broad and bustling High Street, and the colourful wharves of its canal only a short distance westwards.

The castle dates back to Norman times, but most of the existing structure is the work of the Clifford family, who acquired it in 1311. Damaged in the Civil War it was repaired by Lady Anne Clifford, who also added a balustrade between the two massive towers of the gatehouse incorporating the family motto *'Desormais'* (Henceforth). We were delighted to encounter a most cheerful and helpful custodian here, and were handed a very useful leaflet with forty sketches providing a step by step guide to this exceptionally interesting building. See especially the 'Long Drop', a 'typical example of early sanitation' and the charming Conduit Court, shaded by a yew planted during Lady Anne's restoration in 1659.

The church is a largely Perpendicular building, and this was also extensively restored by Lady Anne. See especially the 14th century four seater sedilia, the splendid Jacobean font cover, and the series of Clifford tombs, including the tomb of Lady Anne's father, George Clifford, third Earl of Cumberland, which was erected by her in 1654, almost fifty years after his death.

Having looked at the castle and church, walk down the High Street, visit the Craven Museum (through the town hall entrance) . . . an interesting display of local archaeological and folk items. Turn right and right again, down delightful Coach Street, and over the colourful Springs Canal, which is a spur of the Leeds and Liverpool (see page 29). Turn right, either along the canal, or along the main road beyond, and return to the area of the church.

Leeds and Liverpool Canal (see page 29)

1. Steam at Embsay Station

2. Skipton Castle

3. Conduit Court, Skipton Castle

4. Quiet moorings at Skipton

Map 5

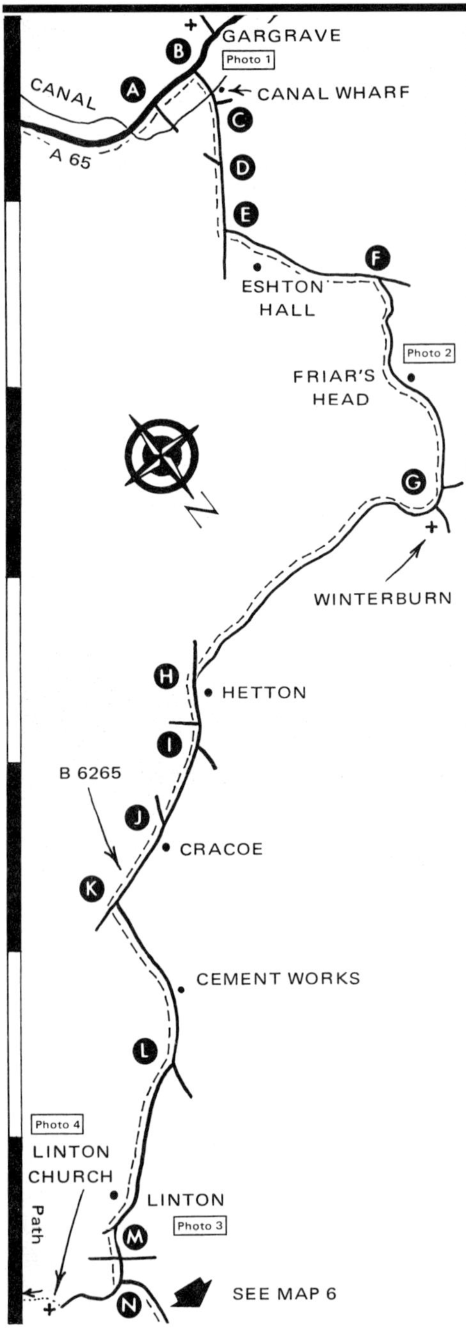

Ref.	Miles	Directions	Sign-posted
	1.6	Over two bridges crossing canal and river	
		Gargrave entry signed	
A	.2	Straight, not right by lay-by	No sign
B	.1	Turn right, off A65 (But go straight ahead if you wish to visit Gargrave)	Malham
	.2	Over canal by lock	
C	.1	Straight, not left	No sign
D	.3	Straight, not right	Malham
E	.4	Bear left, and through old gate pillars	Airton
	.2	Eshton Hall on right	
F	.8	Turn right, beyond bend by Eshton House	Winterburn
	.3	Over small bridge	
	.4	Friar's Head on left (house)	
G	.6	Straight, not left, by old bridge, and...	Hetton
		Fork right in Winterburn (Chapel in field to left)	Hetton
	1.7	Enter Hetton, and...	
		Bear round to left, and...	No sign
H		Straight, not right at Y junction	Cracoe
	.1	The Angel Inn on left	
I	.2	Straight, not right at T junction	Cracoe
	.1	Fork right	Cracoe
	.2	Over small level-crossing	
	.4	Cracoe entry signed	
J	.2	Bear left, on to B6265	Grassington
	.3	Devonshire Arms on right	
K	.2	Bear left, keeping on B6265	Grassington
	.7	Vast quarry complex on left	
L	.4	Fork right, on to narrower road	Linton
	.2	Over railway bridge	
	.6	Linton entry signed	
		Linton Manor on left	
	.1	Village green on right	
	.1	Over bridge	
	.1	Fork left, keeping on wider road	No sign
M	.2	Over X rds., crossing B6160 (We are now in Wharfedale)	Linton Falls
N	.1	Bear left at T junction, and... (But turn down right if you wish to visit Linton Church, etc. — .3)	No sign
		Over Bow Bridge, crossing River Wharfe	
	.1	Old School building on left	
		Total mileage on this map: 11.3	

On Route

Gargrave

Large village astride the busy A59, with wide greens and pleasant tree clad banks beside the River Aire. Well beyond the old stone bridge the church sits beside a quiet road southwards. It is a well proportioned Victorian building, with a Perpendicular tower. The interior contains very little of interest apart from the fragments of at least two Angle-Saxon crosses. To the north of the village, is a quiet wharf on the Leeds and Liverpool Canal, which must have once been busy with the shipping of lead from the mines of Wharfedale. The Pennine Way which we shall encounter later, passes through Gargrave.

Friar's Head Hall

Beautiful 17th century house in a quiet setting in the valley of the Eshton Beck, built on the site of a grange of Furness Abbey. Sir Stephen Procter, builder of Fountains Hall (see page 5) was born here.

Winterburn

Quiet hamlet with a few farms, an old single arch bridge, and a delightful 17th century 'Independent' church. . . one of the earliest non-conformist buildings in the country. It has diamond panelled windows and painted pews, and from our road could easily be mistaken for a small farmhouse.

Hetton

A tidy village with pleasant views across to the crags on Cracoe Fell, but no other special features apart from the hospitable Angel Inn.

Cracoe

Long village astride the straight B6265, with prosperous houses, a small inn (the Devonshire Arms), and an obelisk far up on Cracoe Fell. . . a memorial to those who fell in the two great wars. The less said about the great quarry works beyond, the better. . . let us move on to Linton.

Linton

A little monument on the green commemorates Linton's victory of the News Chronicle's 'Prettiest Village in the North' competition in 1949. . . a doubtful privilege, but one can still appreciate the judges' reasons. Here is a tree shaded green, with a small stream crossed by a clapper bridge, a packhorse bridge and a ford, all overlooked by a series of pleasant buildings. At the far end is Fountaine's Hospital, a dignified range of 18th century almshouses, with a facade so impressive that it has been ascribed to Vanbrugh. Nearby is the friendly Fountaine Inn, 17th century Linton Hall, and 'White Abbey'. . . a delightful 17th century house overlooking Bow Bridge from our left.

Linton Church

A charming little building beside the River Wharfe, with a most unusual bell turret at its west end. We were delighted with the interior, which has been restored with great sensitivity. . . see especially

continued on page 29

1. The River Aire at Gargrave

2. Friar's Head Hall, near Winterburn

3. Summertime at Linton

4. West belfry, Linton Church

Map 6

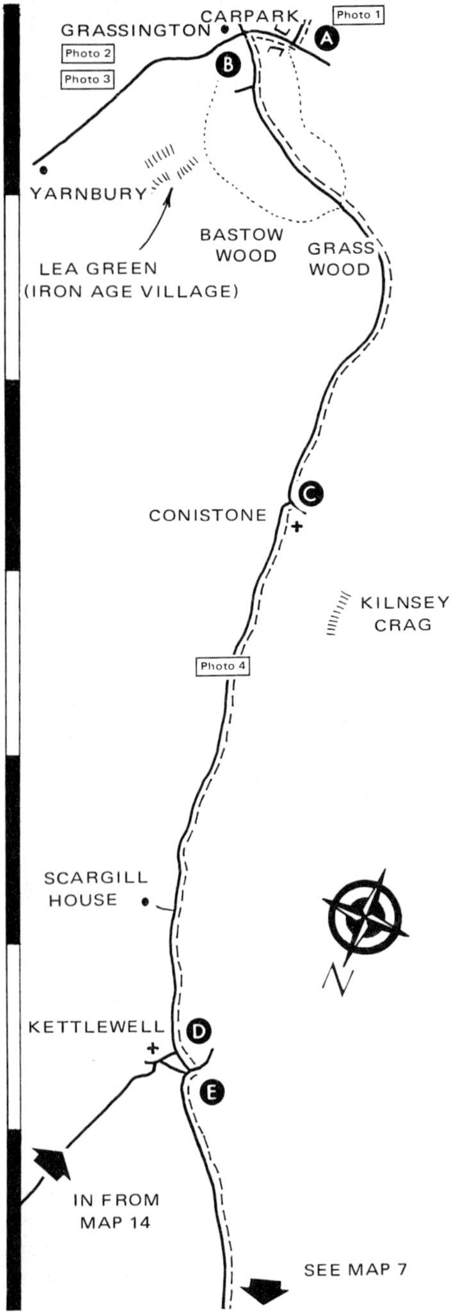

kms Ref.	Miles	Directions	Sign-posted
	.2	Pleasant views over River Wharfe, across to Grassington	
A	.1	Turn right, on to B6265	Grassington
	.1	Cross large stone bridge over River Wharfe at entry to Grassington	
B	.2	Turn left at off-set X rds in village (But turn right on to B6265, Hebden Road for large car park and National Park Centre, on right after a few yards) (But go straight ahead up through village if you wish to explore up to Yarnbury and Grassington Moor — 1.7)	Conistone
	.3	Straight, not right	No sign
	.8	Into Grass Wood... a large wooded area	
	.4	Views of River Wharfe down through trees to left	
	.4	Kilnsey Crag visible far ahead left	
	.9	Enter Conistone	
C	.1	Bear right at T junction in Conistone	No sign
		Church on left	
	.3	Kilnsey Crag now across dale to left	
	2.2	Driveway to Scargill House on right	
	.5	Old mine road climbing up beyond Kettlewell, visible ahead right	
	.2	Enter Kettlewell	
D	.1	Bear left at T junction by Police Station	Buckden
		(WE ARE JOINED HERE FROM THE END OF MAP 14)	
E	.1	Turn right, with care on to B6160 (But turn left if you wish to park)	Buckden
		Racehorses Hotel on left	
		Bluebell Hotel on right	
		Total mileage on this map: 6.9	

On Route

Grassington

Cross over Grassington Bridge, a fine stone structure built in 1603 and widened in 1784. . . and up into Grassington. Do not try to park in the centre, but use the park on the Hebden Road (see Route Directions), where there is an interesting National Park Centre. Then walk back and explore up into the delightful cobbled market place, and up the steep sloping streets beyond. Here will be found a wide choice of shops, hotels, inns and restaurants, for Grassington is one of the chief tourist centres of the Dales and undisputed queen of upper Wharfedale. Its importance dates from the opening of the Yorkshire Dales Railway from Skipton in 1902, and although this was closed to passenger traffic in 1930, Grassington's popularity has continued to grow apace. Do not miss a visit to the interesting little Folk Museum.

A short distance to the north west (walk up Chapel Street from Town Hall) are the bumpy earthworks of an Iron Age village and its attendant field system, in an area known as Lea Green. It is possible to walk from here to Bastow Wood and Grass Wood, where one can re-join our route, or walk back to Grassington along the banks of the Wharfe.

Diversion to Grassington Moor

Drive up straight through Grassington from Point B for 1.7 miles, to the mining settlement of Yarnbury on high Grassington Moor. A short distance beyond are splendid views over the moors and a wealth of industrial remains. . . reminders of Grassington Moor's past importance as a lead mining area, at least since Roman times. Great care should be taken when exploring this area as many mine shafts are inadequately fenced off.

Grass Wood

Contains many rare botanical specimens. Please leave the area undisturbed and do not pick any wild flowers.

Conistone

Small village beneath the high limestone cliffs of Conistone Pie and Wassa, looking across Wharfedale to Kilnsey Crag, a dramatic overhanging rock face (see Book 1). The little Norman church is well sited above the valley and although considerably 'neo-Normanised' by the Victorians, it retains its original arcading and chancel arch.

Kettlewell

Once prosperous from lead mining on the fells above it, Kettlewell is now a busy little tourist centre, with three small hotels overlooking a bridge over the little Park Gill Beck, and the King's Head by the church. Set in an attractive churchyard, this is largely of 19th century origin, but there are several items of interest within, including a Norman font, two stained-glass windows from the studios of William Morris, and a fine east window depicting troops resting in the trenches on the eve of the Battle of the Somme. The altar is of English oak, by Colin Almack, a pupil of Robert Thompson, the Kilburn 'mouse' man (see also Hubberholme, page 15). Almack's own symbol is a beaver, but there is a Thompson mouse nearby.

1. The Wharfe below Grassington Bridge

2. In Grassington Square

3. Bow fronts at Grassington

4. Wharfedale north from Conistone

Map 7

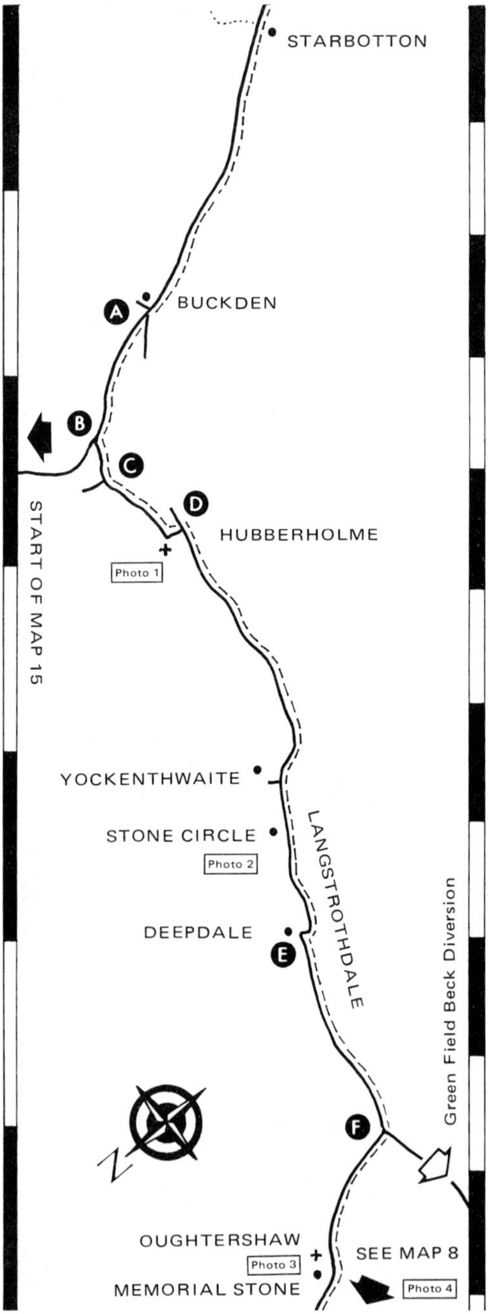

Ref.	Miles	Directions	Sign-posted
	1.7	Starbotton entry signed (Keep straight through Starbotton)	
	.2	Fox and Hounds Inn on right	
	1.4	Buckden entry signed	
	.2	Attractive modern housing development on left	
A	.1	Over small X rds. beyond the Buck Inn	Aysgarth
	.1	Large car park up to right	
B	.6	Fork left, off B6160... watch for this narrow road with care (BUT GO STRAIGHT AHEAD ON B6160 IF YOU WISH TO START MAP 15)	Hubberholme
C	.3	Bear left, and over small bridge	No sign
D	.5	Bear left, and over bridge by Hubberholme church, and... Turn right by the George Inn (Now in Langstrothdale)	No sign
	1.4	Over cattle-grid, on to open country	
	.2	Yockenthwaite Farm over to right	
	.4	Excellent picnic opportunities beside stream to right of road. Small Bronze Age stone circle over wall beyond stream on right	
E	.5	Turn right, and over bridge at Deepdale	No sign
		Now climbing steadily up beside stream	
F	1.1	Fork right at Y junction (But fork left if you wish to explore up valley of the Green Field Beck)	Hawes
	.8	Oughtershaw old church on right	
	.2	Memorial stone on left	
		Now climbing up away from valley	
		NOW OFF MAP	
	1.1	Splendid views of Ingleborough over to far left	
	.7	Good parking space on right	
G	.7	Bear right at T junction (But turn left if you wish to follow course of Roman road almost as far as Cam Houses — 3 miles)	Hawes
	.1	Fine views ahead of Great Shunner Fell and Lovely Seat	
	.3	1 in 4 descent signed ENGAGE LOW GEAR	
H	.1	Course of Roman road bears off to right, as we start our descent	
	.7	Mine spoil heaps on both sides of road	
	1.0	Through Scar Head hamlet	
		Total mileage on this map: 14.6	

On Route

Starbotton

Small village set in Wharfedale, with an old road to the right leading up to long disused lead mines on the fells. There is an attractive little inn, the Fox and Hounds, and several well restored houses.

Buckden

This is set in the deep northern confines of Wharfedale, and is overlooked by high Buckden Pike (2302′). Above a small green is the Buck Inn, an old coaching house with the deer upon its sign reminding us that Buckden was once the headquarters of Langstrothdale Chase, a medieval hunting preserve with its own 'forest laws'.

Hubberholme

Here between the steep wooded slopes of Langstrothdale, is a cheerful inn, the George, looking across a small bridge to an interesting church with Norman origins. It is a very wide building with a squat tower and a wonderfully unspoilt interior. This contains modern pews. . . each with a little carved mouse. . . the 'signature' of Robert Thompson, of Kilburn and a rare and beautiful 16th century rood loft and screen with delicately pierced tracery.

Yockenthwaite

Here is an old pack-horse bridge overlooked by a very attractive farmhouse, and about 700 yards to the north west (see Route Directions) a small, but well preserved Bronze Age stone circle.

Langstrothdale

Beyond Yockenthwaite our road follows close to the Wharfe up this most delightful dale, often with open grassland between road and river. These delectable picnic places are much used on Sundays, but are still relatively quiet on weekdays.

Green Field Diversion

Fork left at Point F if you wish to explore up this valley for a certain distance by car. Eventually the tarred section comes to an end, but it is possible to walk over to Birkwith Moor, linking on to the Pennine Way, and then head south to Horton-in- Ribblesdale. Do not attempt this without O.S. map.

Oughtershaw

This pretty hamlet is tucked away at the head of Langstrothdale, with a few old cottages overlooking the infant Wharfe, and a simple memorial inscribed VR 1887. . . no doubt commemorating Queen Victoria's jubilee.

Cam Houses Diversion

If you wish to follow the course of a Roman road which ran from Brough-by-Bainbridge to Ingleton, turn left at Point G. It is possible to drive along this high mountain road for three miles, and there are splendid views down to Langstrothdale and, on a clear day, ahead to the dramatic outline of Ingleborough. This is one of the rare occasions when we share a length of route with the Pennine Way.

1. Hubberholme Church

2. Stone Circle beyond Yockenthwaite

3. Oughtershaw

4. Descent into Sleddale

Map 8

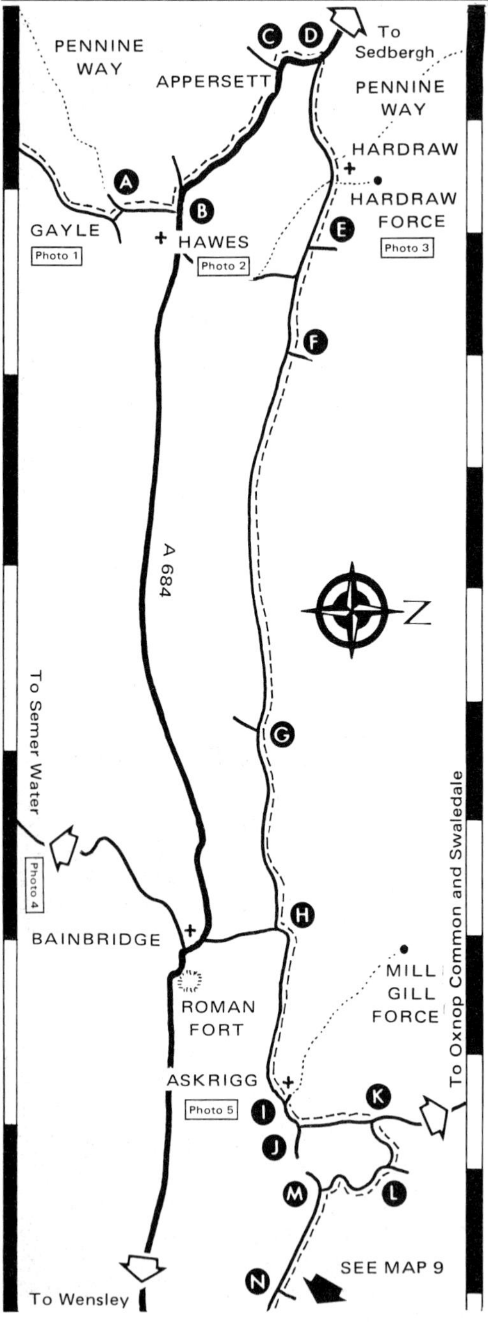

Ref.	Miles	Directions	Sign-posted
	.8	Gayle entry signed	
		Down 1 in 6 hill	
	.2	Parking space on left beside ford	
A	.1	Turn left, over bridge, and...	Hawes
		Bear right beyond bridge	Hawes
		Now entering Hawes	
B	.3	Turn left, on to A684 (But turn right if you wish to visit Hawes)	Sedbergh
	.1	Bear right, keeping on A684	Sedbergh
	.8	Appersett entry signed	
C	.2	Bear right, over bridge, keeping on A684, and...	No sign
	.1	Over second bridge, and...	
D	.1	Turn right, off A684	Hardraw
	.6	Hardraw entry signed	
	.1	Over bridge	
		Green Dragon Inn on left. (Go through inn to visit Hardraw Force)	
E	.5	Straight, not left at T junction	Hawes
	.1	Straight, not right at T junction	Askrigg
F	.5	Straight, not left	No sign
		Pleasant open road with views of Wensleydale over to right	
G	2.1	Straight, not right	No sign
H	1.2	Bear left at T junction (But turn right if you wish to visit Bainbridge — .3, and/or Semer Water — 3 miles)	Askrigg
	.8	Askrigg entry signed	
I	.2	Bear round to right by war memorial and church	No sign
		Path to Mill Gill Force signed to left	
J	.2	Bear left, off wider road in Askrigg, and...	Muker
	.1	Up 1 in 4 hill	
K	.3	Turn right at T junction (But go straight ahead if you wish to go over Oxnop Common to Swaledale (linking on to Book 1), 4 miles)	Reeth
L	.3	Fork right, keeping on lower road	No sign
	.1	Fine views of Wensleydale ahead	
M	.5	Bear left, on to wider road	No sign
N	.7	Straight, not left at T junction	No sign
		Total mileage on this map: 11.0	

On Route

Sleddale

Beyond page 14, Point H our road drops steeply down into Sleddale and there are fine views of Wensleydale ahead, with glimpses of the road climbing out beyond towards the Buttertubs Pass (see Book I).

Gayle

Small village to the immediate south of Hawes, with its waterfalling stream crossed by an attractive old bridge and a wide ford. This is a chunky, compact little place with several pleasant houses overlooking the stream, and a modern creamery producing that delicious Wensleydale cheese.

Hawes

Busy little Hawes derives its name from the Norse word 'hause'. . . a pass through the mountains, and a word still used in the Lake District. It is in fact the highest market town in Yorkshire and the second highest in England. It is THE tourist centre for upper Wensleydale, but its continuing significance as a market town has ensured that its flavour survives. The church was built by the Victorians and is not of great interest to visitors, but Hawes will always be remembered for its multitude of bustling shops, restaurants and inns, and its lovely setting at the upper end of Wensleydale. The converted railway station contains a National Park Centre and the Dales Countryside Museum, which houses the fascinating collection of old Dales material formed by Marie Hartley and Joan Ingilby. Also do not miss 'The Hawes Ropemakers' in Town Foot, where visitors are welcome to watch ropes made by the traditional method.

Hardraw

Minute village with a modest Victorian church and a hotel called the Green Dragon Inn. To visit the dramatic 96 feet high Hardraw Force waterfall (claimed to be England's highest above ground), pay a small fee at the Green Dragon and walk through the inn and up beside the stream (about six minutes). This waterfall is impressive after heavy rain and brave souls can walk behind the water and return down the other side of the stream. The accoustic properties of the gorge below the fall made it a favourite place for village band contests in times gone by, and happily these have now been revived.

Bainbridge

Charming village spreading around an exceptionally wide green. On its north side stands the Rose and Crown . . . a cheerful place in whose entrance hall stands Bainbridge's 'Forest Horn'. This is blown each evening in winter at nine . . . a survival of a custom dating back to Bainbridge's connection with the Forest of Wensley, a medieval hunting reserve.

At Brough to the east of the village, are the earthworks of a Roman fort (on private ground), from whence two roads ran southwards (see Cam Houses, page 15, and Kidstones Pass, page 31). Both still provide excellent fell walks.

Semer Water, Askrigg and Oxnop Common (see page 19)

1. Waterfalls at Gayle

2. Cobblestones at Hawes

3. Hardraw Force

4. Wind Force 4 at Semer Water

5. Askrigg Church

Map 9

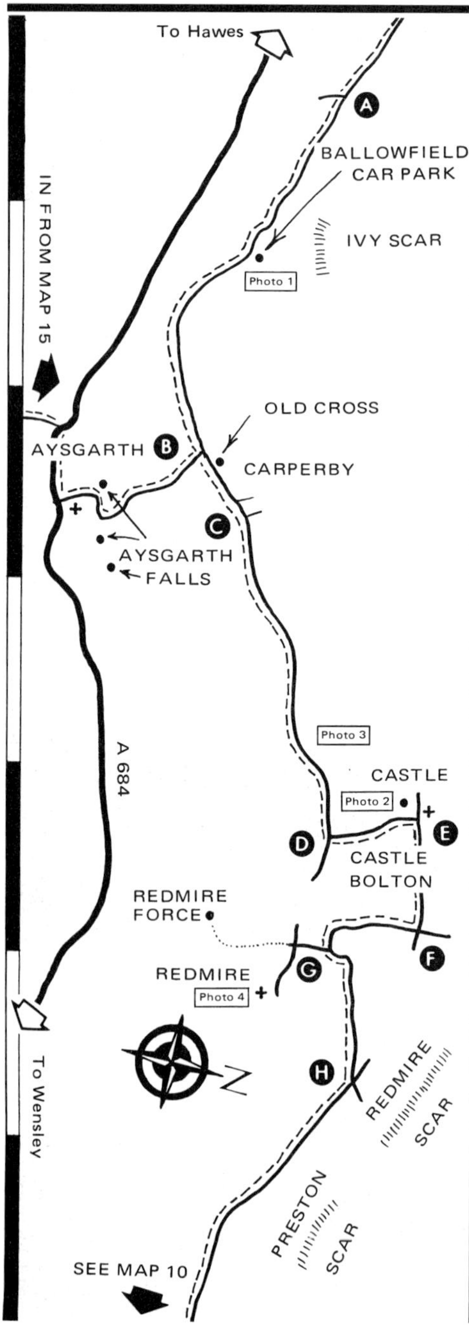

Ref.	Miles	Directions	Sign-posted
	.7	Ivy Scar visible ahead	
A	.2	Straight, not right	No sign
	.6	Attractive streamside on left	
	.2	Car Park on left... Ballowfield area	
	.6	Path to Aysgarth on right	
B	.7	Straight, not right, at entry to Carperby	Castle Bolton
		(WE ARE JOINED HERE FROM THE END OF MAP 15)	
	.1	Wayside cross on left	
	.2	Wheatsheaf Inn on left	
C		Straight, not left twice near end of village	No sign
	.6	Chimney on skyline ahead... a reminder of lead mining activity between Bolton and Grinton in 18th and 19th centuries	
	.1	Bolton Castle visible ahead	
D	1.3	Turn left at T junction	Castle Bolton
	.3	Over course of old railway line	
	.1	Castle Bolton entry signed	
	.2	Castle on left, and...	
E		Turn right at T junction (But turn left if you wish to visit castle)	Redmire
	.5	Over bridge in woodlands crossing Apedale Beck	
F	.2	Turn right at T junction	Redmire
	.2	Under railway bridge, and...	
		Enter Redmire	
	.2	Bolton Arms on right, and...	
G	.1	Fork left by village green, and... (But fork right, bear right and turn left if you wish to visit church — .4)	No sign
		Straight, not right	Leyburn
	.4	Under railway bridge	
H	.5	Straight, not left	Wensley
		Total mileage on this map: 8.0	

On Route

Semer Water (see page 16)

This is Yorkshire's largest natural lake, and is an all too popular place for boating, fishing and picnicking. It is in a delightful bowl-like setting in the hills and has a small stony beach at its southern end.

Askrigg (see page 16)

Until the building of the new turnpike to Lancaster in 1795, Askrigg was the market centre of upper Wensleydale, but it has now long since been superseded in this respect by Hawes, through which the turnpike ran. In the eyes of most visitors this isolation has certainly been Askrigg's gain, for it is a charming place. . . small, compact, town-like, and utterly different from widespread Bainbridge. The fine Perpendicular church, overlooking a small cobbled 'square', has a slender tower, broad aisles and beautiful nave roof. . . one of the best in the dales. A path just beyond the church leads to 70′ high Mill Gill Force (waterfall).

Oxnop Common (see page 16)

Go straight ahead at Point K, if you wish to take the exhilarating moorland road over Oxnop Common, below Oxnop Scar and down into Swaledale linking with Book 1, Map 8, Point F. . . a distance of 4 miles.

Carperby

Long tidy village with a 17th century market cross (market charter granted 1303) on a heavily stepped base, a warm little inn, the Wheatsheaf, and pastoral views out over Wensleydale.

Castle Bolton

A pleasant small village with wide greens and a late 14th century church with a low tower. The village was almost certainly established at the same time as the splendid Bolton Castle. This was built in the late 14th century by Richard Scrope, Lord Chancellor to Richard II, the first Baron Bolton; and it is regarded by Professor Nikolaus Pevsner as 'a climax of English military architecture'. It is a building of great romantic quality, (enhanced by Mary Queen of Scots' captivity here in 1568), and it must have dominated Wensleydale most effectively. The interior is full of interest and includes 'Queen Mary's Bedroom', a chapel, a dungeon, a small museum and a replica of a 19th century 'Dales Kitchen'.

Redmire

Charmingly sited around widespread greens, with two inns, the Bolton Arms and the King's Arms; and a small church tucked away about half a mile down a quiet lane. This was originally a chantry chapel, but at the Reformation it became the parish church (Redmire had previously been in Wensley parish). It has a Norman south door, a Perpendicular east window and a pleasant old roof.

It is possible to walk down from the village to Redmire Force. . . beautiful waterfalls on the wide River Ure (half a mile due south). (Take road towards church, but go out over small crossroads instead of turning left for the church.)

1. Stream beside Ballowfield Car Park

2. Bolton Castle

3. Wensleydale from Castle Bolton

4. At Redmire

Map 10

Miles

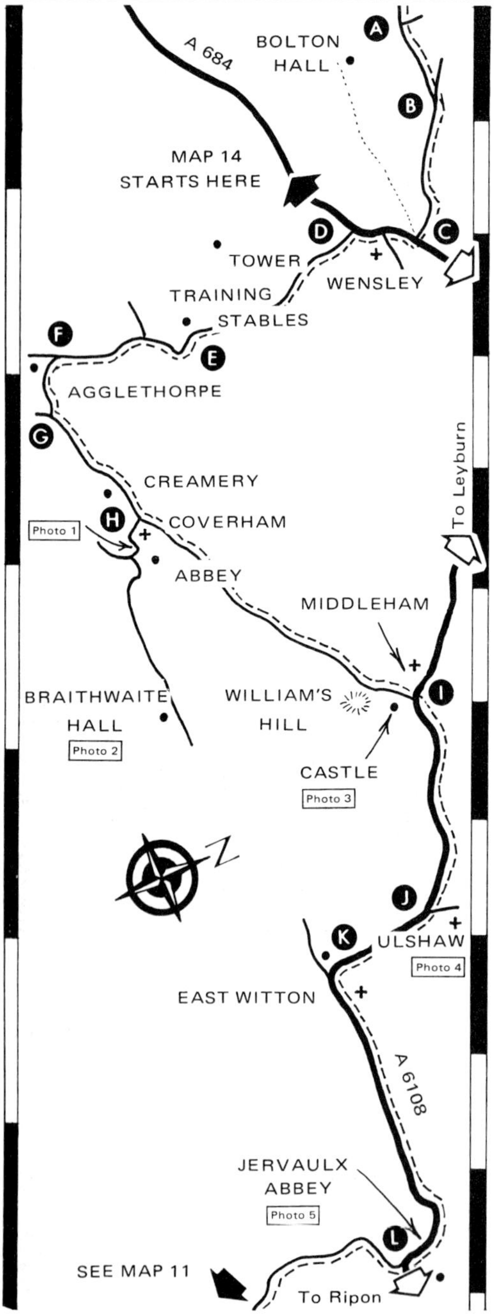

kms Ref. Miles

Ref.	Miles	Directions	Sign-posted
A	.8	Straight, not left	Wensley
	.2	Over railway bridge	
B	.8	Bear right at Y junction, keeping on wider road	No sign
	.7	Enter Wensley	
C	.1	Turn right with care on to A684	West Witton
		Three Horseshoes Inn on left, and car park for Wensley Mill	
	.1	Straight, not left, by church, keeping on A684	West Witton
	.1	Over bridge, crossing River Ure	
D	.2	Turn left, off A684 (BUT GO STRAIGHT AHEAD ON A684 IF YOU WISH TO START MAP 13)	Carlton
	.1	Ruined tower just visible ahead right	
	.2	Now climbing out of Wensleydale	
	.8	Training stables entrance on right	
E	.2	Bear sharp right, up hill	No sign
	.2	Bear left at T junction beyond National Park entry sign	Carlton
	.2	Pleasant views ahead, up Coverdale	
F	.2	Turn left in Agglethorpe hamlet	Coverham
G	.5	Bear left at T junction, on to wider road	No sign
	.5	Creamery on right	
H	.2	Straight, not right, by lych gate to Coverham church (But turn right, cross Coverham Bridge and bear left if you wish to visit Braithwaite Hall — 1.2)	Middleham
	.7	Small lake on left, and open country beyond. Beware of race horses at exercise	
	.8	Middleham entry signed	
	.1	Earthworks of old castle (William's Hill) up to right	
	.2	Middleham Castle to right	
I	.2	Straight, not left, joining A6108	Masham
J	1.2	Bear right by the Coverbridge Inn, keeping on A6108, and over bridge (But turn left if you wish to look at Ulshaw Bridge — .1)	Masham
	.6	East Witton entry signed	
K	.1	Bear left by green	Bedale
	.1	Church on left	
	1.6	Jervaulx Abbey over to left. Car Park on right	
L	.2	Bear right at T junction, WITH GREAT CARE, leaving A6108	Ellingstring
		Total mileage on this map: 11.9	

On Route

Wensley

An important market town in medieval times, Wensley is today little more than an estate village beside the elegant gates of Bolton Hall (*partly re-built in 1902 following a disastrous fire . . . not open to the public*). It is a neat, tidy place, with church and cottages looking over a trim green, and a cosy little inn, the Three Horseshoes, modestly tucked away from the road. Wensley's fine church tower was re-built in the 18th century, but the medieval details in chancel, two storeyed vestry, aisles and porches are full of interest. The lofty interior is a treasure house of beautiful things, among them a triple sedilia, a Flemish brass to Simon Wensley, rector 1361 – 94, and the Bolton family pew, still hung with rich fabrics and backed by a parclose screen brought from the family chantry chapel at Easby Abbey.

Coverham

Here is a simple Victorianised church in an overgrown churchyard, and below it, a little mill house, with a beautiful medieval bridge just beyond. This was probably built by the monks of Coverham Abbey, little of which now remains. Prints of the abbey, pottery and a large selection of plants are available at the adjoining nursery.

Braithwaite Hall (NT)

Stout 17th century 'hall', now a working farmhouse, and owned by the National Trust. Its pleasant and interesting interior is open only by arrangement with the tenant.

Middleham

Once the administrative centre of Wensleydale and an important market town, Middleham is now best known for the breeding and training of racehorses. The great castle of Middleham came into the hands of the powerful Neville family in the 13th century, and passed by marriage to Richard III. It fell into ruins after the Civil War, but it remains today as an impressive reminder of feudal times. The market town itself is centred around the sloping Market Square below the castle. The church has several interesting features including some beautifully restored Victorian mural paintings.

Ulshaw Bridge

Beautiful 17th century bridge, with cut-waters, one of which houses a little sundial, dated 1674. The nearby Roman Catholic church is highly reminiscent of provincial France.

East Witton

A charming 'estate village' re-built in 1809, with cottages looking out over flower filled gardens to an elongated green. The church was built at the same date . . . a solid neo-Gothic piece of work.

Jervaulx Abbey

The Cistercians established an abbey here in 1156, having made a false start at Fors near Aysgarth eleven

continued on page 23

1. Coverham Bridge

2. Braithwaite Hall

3. Middleham Castle

4. Ulshaw Church

5. At Jervaulx Abbey

Map 11

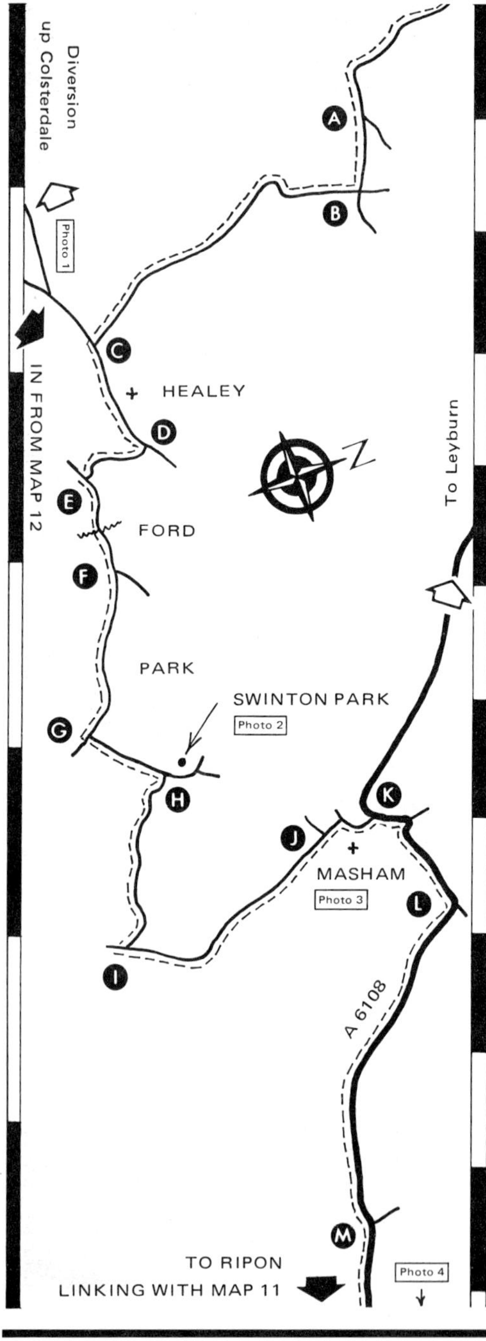

Ref.	Miles	Directions	Sign-posted
	.8	Climb steep hill	
A	.7	Straight, not left	No sign
B	.4	Turn right at X rds.	No sign
C	2.0	Turn left at T junction and... (But turn right and fork right to explore up Colsterdale — 4 miles) WE ARE JOINED HERE FROM THE END OF MAP 12)	Healey
		Healey entry signed	
	.3	Church on left	
D	.3	Fork right at Y junction	Swinton
	.5	Over bridge in pleasantly wooded valley, and...	
E		Bear left at T junction	Swinton
		Attractive stream with trees on left	
	.2	Through ford	
F	.3	Fork right by estate wall	No sign
G	1.0	Turn left at T junction	No sign
H	.5	Turn right at small T junction just before cottages on right WATCH FOR THIS WITH CARE (But go straight ahead to look at Swinton Park — .2)	No sign
	.9	Into open country with picnic possibilities	
I	.2	Turn sharp left on to wider road	Masham
	1.0	Over bridge crossing River Burn	
J	.4	Straight, not left	Bedale
	.2	Bear round to right by Midland Bank, and...	No sign
		Bear left in square	Tanfield
		Church over to right	
K	.1	Bear right on to A6108 (Keep on A6108 for 10 miles... into Ripon)	Ripon
	.2	Over fine old bridge, crossing River Ure	
	.1	Bear right	Tanfield
L	.6	Bear right	Tanfield
M	1.4	Straight, not left	No sign
		NOW OFF MAP	
	1.2	Bear left at entry to Tanfield Church and gatehouse over to right	North Stainley
	.3	Turn right	Ripon
	.1	Over River Ure	
	1.0	Straight, not right, twice	Ripon
	.1	North Stainley entry signed	
	.3	Church on right	
	.4	North Stainley Hall on right	
	2.9	Enter Ripon	
	.6	Bear right on to A61, by clock tower	Harrogate
	.4	Arrive Ripon Market Square, LINKING WITH MAP 1, POINT A, by turning right at end of square	
		Total mileage on this page: 19.4	

On Route

Jervaulx Abbey *continued from page 21*
years earlier. The last abbot, one of the leaders of the ill-fated Pilgrimage of Grace, was hanged at Tyburn in 1537, and the abbey was dissolved in the same year. The highly atmospheric ruins are in private hands, but are open to the public.

Colsterdale (see page 29)

Healey

Here is a row of cottages with colourful gardens, looking southwards over richly wooded Colsterdale. The little cruciform church, with central spire, was built in 1848 but its interior is not of great interest to visitors.

Swinton Park

Only a distant glimpse of the castellated early 19th century front may be obtained through the handsome 'East Gates' (*divert at Point H*). The splendours of the great park, with its woods, lakes and streams, are unfortunately hidden behind high estate walls. (This is not open to the public.)

Masham

We cross a fine 18th century bridge into Masham, and another of the same period on our road beyond. Between them lies a delightful little town, with an exceptionally spacious Market Place centred upon an old market cross, and overlooked by a series of quietly dignified 17th and 18th century houses. Here also is Uredale Glass, where visitors may see glass being made, and the nearby Theakston Brewery, the source of the noted ale, Old Peculier, has an interesting visitor centre.

Overlooking the Market Place is the large church, with its Norman tower topped by a 15th century spire. Near the south porch stands part of a cylindrical Anglo- Saxon cross shaft, splendidly ornamented with primitive carved figures. The interior has many items of interest including the charming monument to Sir Marmaduke Wyvill in the south aisle, with two effigies lying stiffly on their sides, and an unusual painting over the chancel arch, thought to be a fragment of a larger work by Sir Joshua Reynolds.

West Tanfield

This village has a fine 18th-century bridge over the broad River Ure, from whence there is a delightful view of the church and the handsome medieval gatehouse beside it. This gatehouse, known as the Marmion Tower and in the care of English Heritage, is situated at the end of a small lane beside the church, and is all that remains of a castle belonging to the Marmion family, several of whom are in effigy upon tomb chests in the church. Do not miss the little chapel built into the supporting wall by the chancel arch ... possibly a chantry chapel for the soul of Maude Marmion, who died in 1335.

North Stainley

Small village astride the A6108, with an unexceptional Victorian church, and a handsome 18th century house set well back from the road . . . North Stainley Hall.

1. Near Colsterdale Head

2. Swinton Park Gates

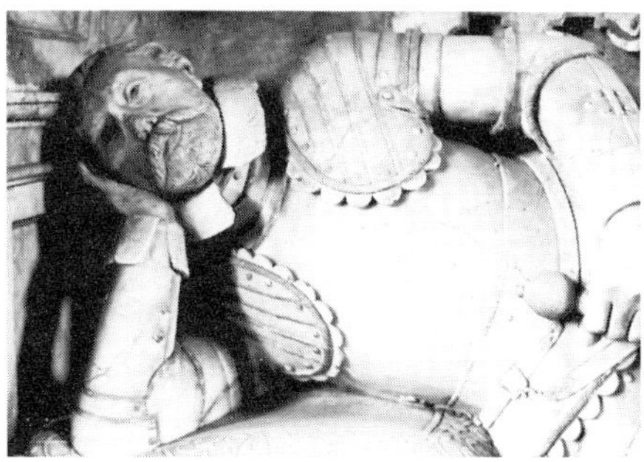

3. Sir Marmaduke Wyvill, Masham

4. Church and Gatehouse, West Tanfield

Miles Map 12

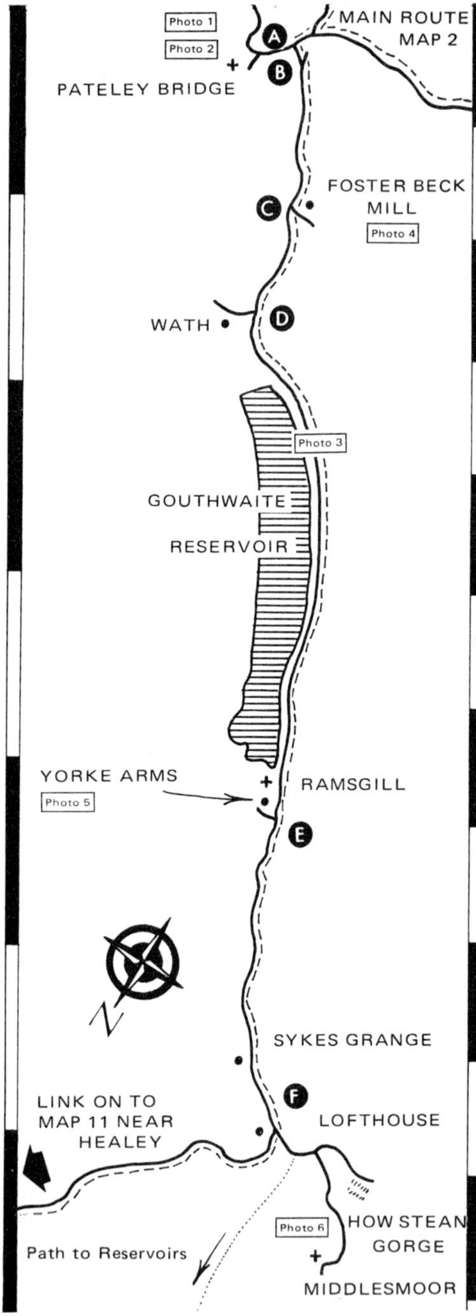

kms Ref.	Miles	Directions	Sign-posted
A		Turn right, on to B6265 by the Royal Oak Inn, Bewerley (THIS IS COMMON WITH MAP 2, POINT I)	Ripon
		Pateley Bridge entry signed, and...	
B	.1	Turn left (But go straight ahead if you wish to visit Pateley Bridge)	Wath
	.9	The Watermill Inn (Foster Beck Mill) on left... note vast waterwheel	
C	.1	Straight, not left	No sign
D	.9	Straight, not right (But walk to right if you wish to visit Wath — .2)	No sign
	.4	Gouthwaite Reservoir just visible to right... now on our right for 2 miles	
	2.3	Ramsgill entry signed	
	.1	Church and Yorke Arms on right	
E	.2	Bear left at T junction beyond bridge	Lofthouse
	.1	River Nidd now on left	
	1.1	Sykes Grange on right	
	.5	Lofthouse entry signed	
F	.2	Turn right at T junction in Lofthouse (But go straight ahead if you wish to explore up to How Stean Gorge — .6 and/or Middlesmoor — 1)	Masham
		Crown Hotel on right	
		Drinking Fountain on right	
		Climb steeply up on to moors beyond Lofthouse	
		NOW OFF MAP	
	1.7	Over the watershead on Jordan Moss, and...	
		Start gradual descent	
	.2	Fine views ahead to north-east	
	2.4	View across Roundhill Reservoir to Arnagill Tower	
	1.6	Leighton Reservoir dam on right	
G	1.8	Bear right and over bridge	No sign
H	.4	Bear right (But turn sharp left if you wish to explore up Colsterdale — 3.6 miles)	Masham
I	.4	Straight, not left at T junction just before entry to Healey (THIS LINKS WITH MAIN ROUTE, AT MAP 11, POINT C)	No sign
		Total mileage on this map: 14.4	

On Route

Pateley Bridge

Attractive little town in Nidderdale, with a touch of 'West Riding industrial' flavour to it. The main street slopes steeply up from the valley, with several details of 18th and early 19th century elegance to be spotted, including bow fronted shop windows and handsome classical porches. The 'new' church was built in 1827, but although it has a pleasantly decorated interior, it is not of great interest to visitors. The ruins of the old church still stand, close to the steep little road leading over the moors to Kirkby Malzeard.

The Mill House Inn, Foster Beck

This is in effect the old Foster Beck flax mill, whose vast cast-iron and timber water wheel was driving machinery up to 1967. Although showing signs of wear last time we called, it has happily so far survived intact.

Wath

Quiet hamlet beneath wooded hillsides with a few houses and a small inn, the Sportsman's Arms. If you wish to visit Wath, please park near point D and walk.

Gouthwaite Reservoir

Long narrow reservoir in Nidderdale, which is an excellent area for bird watching. Wild fowl, usually including Whooper swans, are plentiful in winter.

Ramsgill

The comfortable Yorke Arms Hotel overlooks an exquisite tree shaded green. Houses and cottages are well cared for, with old world gardens and flowering trees, and there is a small early 19th century church. The notorious Eugene Aram (hanged for murder in 1759) was a native of Ramsgill.

Lofthouse

An unexceptional village apart from the quaint verses to be found on its war memorial drinking fountain, which are well worth reading.

How Stean Gorge

Narrow heavily wooded gorge nearly 70′ deep. This lies to the left of our diversion to Middlesmoor and is worth visiting. There are two caves nearby. . . Tom Taylor's Chamber and Eglin's Hole.

Middlesmoor

A splendid little hilltop village, with steep street, small inn, and a cobbled path leading to the church, from whence there are glorious views down over Nidderdale. Completely unspoilt it reminds us of some village in the Tuscan hills. The church is largely Victorian, but its contents include an Anglo-Saxon cross head.

Scar House and Angram Reservoirs

It is possible to walk up the private road from Lofthouse to these two reservoirs at the head of Nidderdale (about 5 miles to Scar House dam). This makes a good starting point for the ascent of Little or Great Whernside, but do not attempt either without adequate equipment or experience.

Colsterdale (see page 29)

1. and 2. Classical elegance at Pateley Bridge

3. Gouthwaite Reservoir

4. The Wheel, Foster Beck Mill

5. Yorke Arms, Ramsgill

6. Nidderdale below Middlesmoor

Map 13

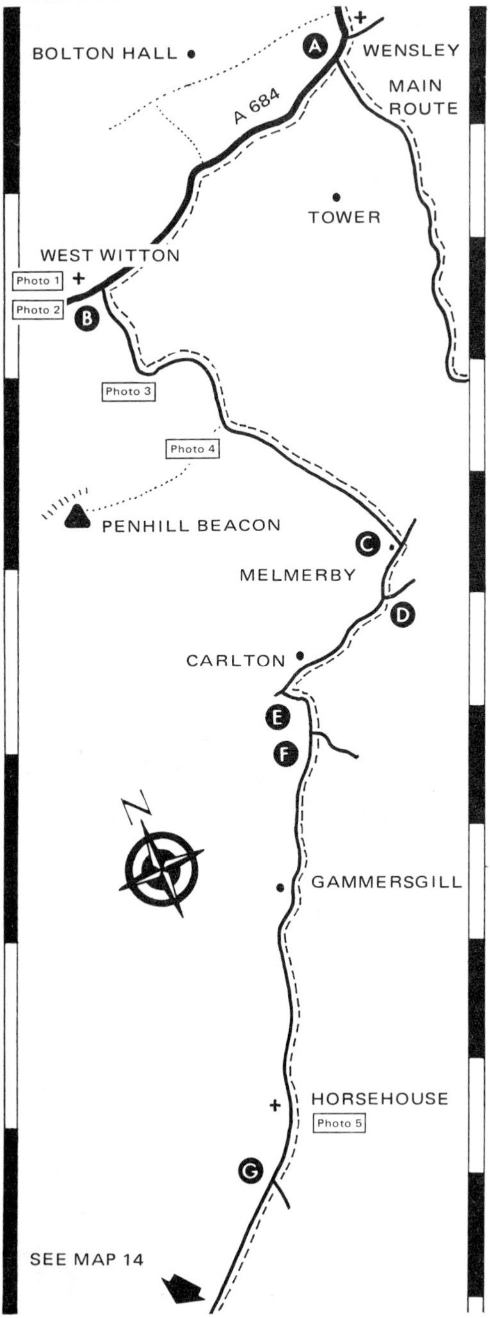

kms Ref.	Miles	Directions	Sign-posted
A		GO STRAIGHT AHEAD ON A684, FROM MAP 10, POINT D, JUST BEYOND WENSLEY	West Witton
	.3	Fine views of Penhill Beacon ahead	
		Ruined tower visible up to left	
	.7	Entrance gates to Bolton Hall on right	
	.6	West Witton entry signed	
B	.3	Turn left, off A684 (But go straight ahead if you wish to visit church, or the Wensleydale Heifer Inn)	Melmerby
	.2	Now climbing steeply out of Wensleydale, with two sharp bends on hill	
	.7	Spendid views back over Wensleydale	
		Turn right at Y junction	Melmerby
	.4	Over cattle-grid on to open moorland	
	.1	Path to Penhill Beacon on right	
	.1	Good views ahead across Coverdale to Scrafton Moor, and on a clear day, over to far left to the North York Moors	
	.2	Start descent towards Coverdale	
	.6	Over cattle-grid at entry to Melmerby	
C	.2	Bear right at T junction	Carlton
D	.4	Bear right at T junction, and...	Carlton
		Carlton entry signed	
	.3	Small Victorian school and chapel on right	
	.1	The Forester's Arms on left	
	.3	Home of Henry Constantine on right (see opposite)	
E	.1	Turn sharp left at end of village	No sign
F	.3	Straight, not left	Kettlewell
	.9	Over small bridge at entry to Gammersgill hamlet	
	.6	Prospect of Coverdale now opening out	
	.6	Horsehouse entry signed The Thwaite Arms on left	
	.1	Church on right	
	.1	Wesleyan chapel on right	
		Little Whernside visible ahead left	
G	.2	Straight, not left (Turn on left is to Arkleside only)	No sign
		Total mileage on this map: 8.4	

On Route

West Witton

Long village astride the A684, with a small church largely re-built in 1875 (apart from the almost inevitable Perpendicular tower). The interior is not of great interest, but there are pleasant views out over Wensleydale from the tree shaded churchyard. We have happy memories of the Wensleydale Heifer Inn. . . an excellent base for exploring the Dales.

Penhill Beacon

Standing at 1727′ above sea level, this windy hilltop provides a splendid viewpoint out over Wensleydale and Coverdale, and is easily climbed from our road (see Route Directions). There was a beacon tower here in Elizabethan times, but all trace of this has vanished long ago.

Carlton

A long village with views out over Coverdale to Scrafton Moor, and a series of attractive stone houses of the 17th and 18th centuries. There are two inns and a house with a stone tablet over the door reminding us that here lived Henry Constantine. . . the 'Coverdale Bard'.

Gammersgill

Several pleasant houses with stone mullioned windows shelter here amongst tall trees on the slopes of Coverdale.

Horsehouse

Here is a delicious terrace of cottages bedecked with colourful little gardens, looking across to the cosy Thwaite Arms. The village shop just beyond looks, in its turn, up to the slim towered Victorian church, the interior of which is relieved only by an unusual wooden chancel arch. Horsehouse probably owes its name to its having been a resting place for packhorses travelling to and fro on our route over to Kettlewell, although it is possible that the Scandinavian word hause may have been involved (see Hawes, page 17). . . it is in any case a charming little place, and well worth visiting.

Ripon *continued from page 3*

A short distance to the east is Ripon's beautiful cathedral, with views of its majestic 'Early English' west front opening up as one walks along the narrow street from the Market Square. St. Wilfrid's monastery church was built about 670, but this was almost entirely destroyed three hundred years later. However St. Wilfrid's Crypt remains below the central tower. . . one of England's oldest Christian survivals. The Norman church, with later medieval additions only became a cathedral in 1836, but it is a fine building containing a wealth of interesting detail. See especially the beautifully restored ceilings beneath the tower and the two transepts, the 15th century crossing screen, the fascinating series of misericords beneath the choir stalls, and of course, St. Wilfrid's crypt.

1. West Witton Church

2. The Wensleydale Heifer, West Witton

3. Wensleydale above West Witton

4. Path to Penhill Beacon

5. Cottages at Horsehouse

Map 14

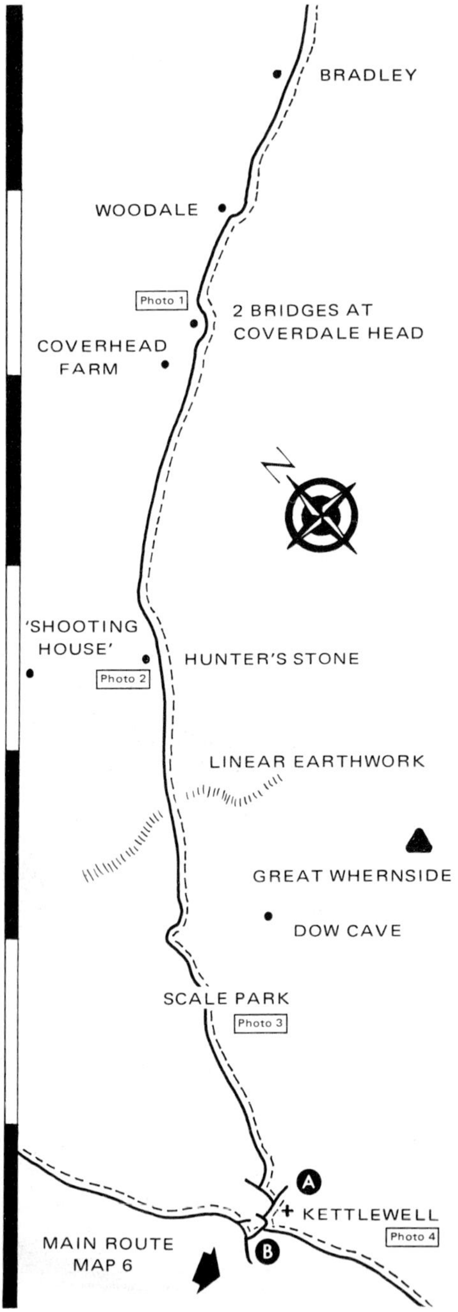

Ref.	Miles	Directions	Sign-posted
	.9	Through Bradley hamlet, and...	
		On to open country	
	.9	The Shooting Lodge, Woodale on right	
	.5	Steep descent... beware of sharp bend to left	
	.2	Over two bridges in valley at Coverdale Head	
		Picnic possibilities between them	
	.4	Over cattle-grid	
		Now climbing out of Coverdale	
	1.2	Small waterfall to left	
	.1	Up steep hill	
	.3	Hunter's Stone on right	
		Old 'Shooting House', visible well over to right	
	.7	Over cattle-grid, crossing linear earthwork following the escarpment	
		Summit of Great Whernside over to left... not very apparent	
	.1	Now starting descent into the dale of Park Gill Beck, which leads into Wharfedale	
	.8	Farmyard on left	
	.1	Fine views of Wharfedale ahead	
		1 in 4 descent signed	
	.2	Down very steep hill with hairpin bends... TAKE VERY GREAT CARE	
	.2	Now in bottom of dale. Park Gill Beck alongside on left	
	1.0	1 in 5 descent with bends signed	
A	.1	Bear round to right at T junction at entrance to Kettlewell	No sign
	.1	Turn left at T junction by Kettlewell Post Office, and... Over bridge, and...	
		Turn right at T junction by King's Head	Skipton
B	.1	Turn right at T junction, near Police Station	Buckden
		(LINKING WITH MAIN ROUTE AT MAP 6, POINT D)	
		Total mileage on this map: 7.9	

On Route

Coverdale Head

Our road crosses the River Cover by a trim little single arch bridge dated 1799, before climbing up, out of the dale towards Hunter's Stone. It was at nearby Coverhead Farm (or Hunter's Hall) that James Metcalfe was born. A ship's carpenter who spent many years on St. Helena, he earned a brief place in history by constructing Napoleon's first coffin.

Hunter's Stone

A solitary, rough stone pillar beside our road, incised with a small cross. This was almost certainly placed here by the monks of Coverham Abbey to mark their route across the moors to Kettlewell.

Great Whernside

The cattle-grid .7 beyond Hunter's Stone marks the old boundary between the North and the West Riding of Yorkshire, and it is interesting to note that the natural scarp has been re-inforced by a man-made linear earthwork (probably thrown up during the Iron Age). Great Whernside summit (2310′)lies less than a mile and a half to the south-east, but it is not visible from this point.

Park Rash

This delightful valley was once a hunting preserve of the Nevilles of Middleham, known as Scale Park. Dow Cave, well over to our left, is for experienced pot holers only.

Colsterdale (see pages 22 & 24)

After climbing over the moors beyond Lofthouse, we drop down into Colsterdale, but turn left at Page 24, Point H, to explore up to the head of the dale road. This is a quiet diversion with only three gates and several opportunities for stream side picnics.

Leeds and Liverpool Canal (see page 8)

Runs 127 miles between Liverpool and Leeds. It was originally surveyed by a Mr. Longbotham, but it was re-surveyed by the famous canal builder, James Brindley, and work commenced in 1770. It was not completed until 1816, but it survives today as one of the country's most attractive and atmospheric canals, and is well worth exploring.

Linton Church *continued from page 11*

the Norman arcading on the north side and the beautifully gilded bosses to the chancel roof.

A few hundred yards beyond the church there are stepping stones across the Wharfe, with paths beyond leading to Hebden and Burnsall, the latter beside the river all the way . . . an attractive walk of about 2ı miles.

1. Bridge at Coverdale Head

2. Hunter's Stone

3. Above Park Gill Beck

4. Kettlewell Church

Map 15

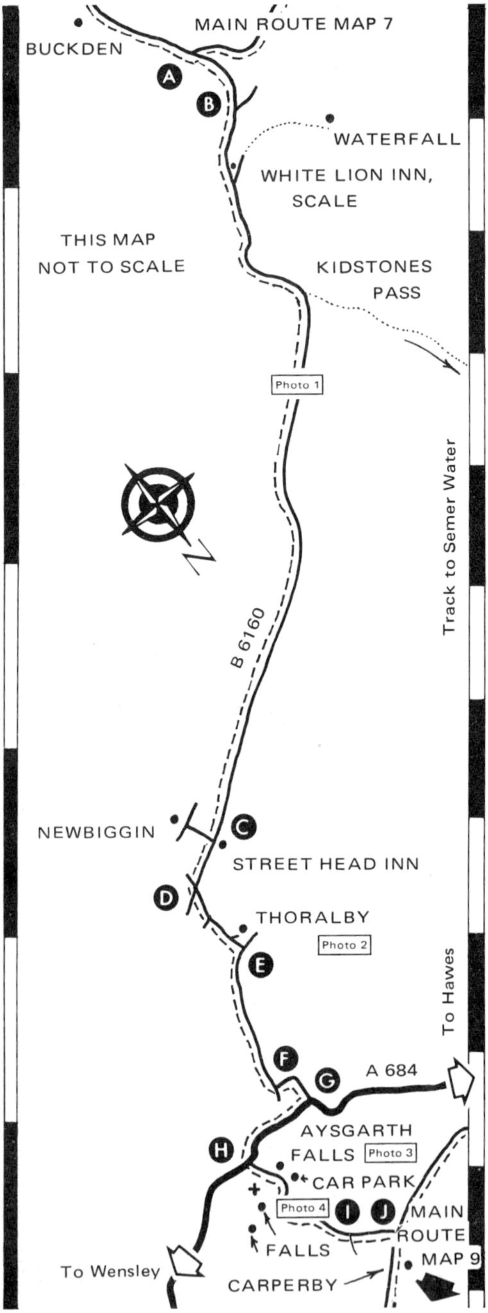

Ref.	Miles	Directions	Sign-posted
A		GO STRAIGHT AHEAD ON B6160, FROM MAP 7, POINT B... (following B6160 for 7 miles)	No sign
B	.5	Straight, not left, keeping on B6160	No sign
	.3	White Lion Inn on left (This is part of Cray hamlet) (Track sharp left behind inn leads to waterfalls)	
	.3	Miniature 'scar' to left	
	.1	Track to left leads over hills to Semer Water	
	.4	Now at head of Kidstones Pass	
	.7	1 in 6 descent signed	
	.1	Bends ahead for 1.75 miles Now dropping down into Bishopdale	
	1.6	Small school on left	
	.6	Over bridge by ruined barn	
	.8	Through hamlet	
	.4	Small 'country cafe' on right	
C	1.1	Straight, not right, by the Street Head Inn	No sign
D	.2	Turn left, at X rds, leaving B6160	Thoralby
	.1	Bear left at T junction and over bridge, and... Thoralby entry signed	Thoralby
	.1	Old corn mill to left	
	.2	Fork right, and...	
E		Bear right Post Office on left	Aysgarth
	.3	Start to climb steeply	
F	.5	Bear left at T junction	No sign
	.1	Aysgarth entry signed	
	.1	Fine views of Wensleydale ahead	
G	.2	Turn right, with care, on to A684 (But go straight ahead if you wish to visit Aysgarth village)	Aysgarth Falls
H	.4	Turn left, off A684, by the Palmer Flatts Hotel	Aysgarth Falls
	.1	Aysgarth church on right Falls visible down left Down steep hill	
	.1	Carriage Museum in old mill on right (But drive on to car park and walk back)	
	.1	Over bridge, with Upper Falls just visible to left	
	.1	Large car park for Aysgarth Falls on left. Also Information Centre and Cafe	
I	.5	Straight, not right	No sign
	.1	Carperby entry signed	
J	.1	Turn right at T junction (LINKING ON TO MAIN ROUTE AT MAP 9, POINT B)	Castle Bolton
		Total mileage on this map: 10.2	

On Route

The White Lion Inn, Cray

This pleasant inn is the only part of Cray hamlet on our road, but if you walk back sharp left, behind the inn, you will pass a few cottages before leaving on a path to some attractive waterfalls.

Kidstones Pass and Bishopdale

Near the summit of Kidstones Pass (1392′) we pass a track to the left which follows the course of the Roman road between Buckden and Bainbridge (see page 17). And now our road goes down into Bishopdale, an elongated, richly agricultural dale with many scattered farmsteads; and villages only at its lower end.

Newbiggin

Large hamlet in Bishopdale with a bridge and cheerful inn on the main road below it. . . the Street Head Inn. Read Harley and Ingilby's 'The Yorkshire Dales' for an account of 'Newbiggin Feast', a three day celebration that appears to have originated with communal sheep washing. We strongly recommend this excellent book to all those who wish to learn more of earlier days in the Dales.

Thoralby

Neat little village looking across Bishopdale to Newbiggin, with a small triangular green. There was a chantry chapel here in medieval times, but all chantry chapels were closed when the monasteries were dissolved, and no trace of this one remains.

Aysgarth

The George and Dragon, a pleasant inn and hotel, stands witness to Aysgarth's former importance as a halt on the Lancaster to York stage coach route. The church lies well away from the village, and is approached down a fine avenue of limes. It is an almost entirely Victorian building and as such is elaborately furnished (see the font, the reredos and the mural on the west wall). However do not miss the reading desk, made up of carved poppy head bench ends, nor the splendid 15th century screen on the south side of the chancel.

The Yorkshire Carriage Museum

(Drive to Aysgarth Falls car park and walk back.) This former water-powered cotton mill, a three-storey-high listed building, was built in 1784. Here will be found a unique collection of Victorian horse-drawn carriages, including a fire-engine, Hansom cab, mail coach, Marston hearse and many others.

Aysgarth Falls

Leave your car in the large car park, once part of Aysgarth Station and visit the handsomely designed National Park Information Centre, before setting off to visit Aysgarth's three beautiful falls on the River Ure. . . Upper, Middle and Lower. . . descending in the course of half a mile between richly wooded banks. . . a fitting climax to our exploration of the glorious Yorkshire Dales.

1. Bishopdale Head

2. At Thoralby

3. Information Centre at Aysgarth Falls

4. Aysgarth Falls

INDEX